C000296339

First published in Great Britain in 2018 by
Scotland Street Press
Edinburgh

www.scotlandstreetpress.com

Cover Design by Bookmark Studio
from an original painting by Petra Reid.

ISBN: 978-1-910895-13-9

Typeset in Scotland by Claire Withers

Printed and bound in Scotland by Airdrie Print Services

**R1**

Twenty-first creatures desiring increase
freeze their breeds, lest they turn tardy, or die;
*you bacterium* halted from decease
brings a self-perfect future memory.
(She'll be my double, but with bigger eyes;
Amazon's shipping five-star *ahem* fuel;
*ne plus ultra*—where kind man's future lies,
lending random sperm your ovum's plain cruel.)
What price hard labour for world's ornament,
how to digitalise mum's gaudy Spring?
I'm streaming my sweet uterine content:
Facebook foetuses rock—quit niggarding!
    Guys! You should preview mini me-to-be
    on nordicdads.com—*like* my wee thee!

**R2**

It's Chriiiiiiiiistmas! Gift me fillers for my brow;
I want baby-bum-smooth, not furrowed field;
three score and ten's like twenty-something now,
tottering old weeds are gagging to be held.
Waste or Waist? Just one of the sad hag lies
Granny passed on in pre-procedure days;
bardies riffed on smiling nips sorry eyes,
lately Loose Womens' boob jobs earn more praise.
See Madge? Wants to be her heir's twin: she'll use
secret A-List docs (still saving for mine)
morphing into Lourdes*–so no excuse
for unbraw breasticles like mine and thine.
　　The longer you're young the shorter you're old:
　　vajazzy your bits up, lest they go cold.

*Lourdes Leon, Madonna's daughter

## R3

I love incarnate me I paid to viewest
evolving in full screen. A.N. Other
and *ex utero's* how I'm renewest:
God bless Science, it is all our mother.
And Mary had an empty little womb
til lo! immaculate winged husbandry
facilitated Jesus out his tomb—
now syringes drip chilled posterity.
To be clear—couriers fast tracked my thee;
why trust Father, Son or Ghost with your prime?
*Dad's* part *anon* in this trinity, see?
Bye Cain, bye Abel. (Who's got the time?)
    Free choice plus market forces: all we be.
    *Junior's* the future of predestined thee.

## R4

It's a mega *cosi fan tutte*\* spend
wiping out the folk's skanky legacy
of looks. I'll go online and get a lend:
payday loans gift me what babes get for free.
Plastic's *fantastic* and not like abuse,
I'm just topping up what Nature should give;
each valentine rose has symmetry's use:
why not sapiens who by selfies live?
We all swipe right so's not to die alone;
visages shan't want filters to deceive
once Fate's lottery of looks is so gone:
lasers clear blood debt parents dare to leave.

    LOL a rose that's me won't compare to thee;
    I'll be worth it, what I can pay to be.


\*What woman wouldn't?

**R5**

Ladytime tags all my physique, this frame
of frailty where insecurities dwell;
overachieving doesn't feel the same;
you've switched feeding on demand for Excel.
Wee, sleekit, digital clocks ticking on
through your maternity log-off; bide there
too long... the job, like river snaw, it's gone—
and BC* career girls run everywhere.
What to do when there's no SMP left?
Studies claim *mum's* lost her urge to smash glass:
but it's a broad brush says we're all bereft
of ambition post-partum; then I was
    grateful for jobs; but home stroke work don't
    meet...
    then lost *careers* taste sour as breast milk's
    sweet.

*Before Children

**R6**

...don't let your man's duff DNA deface
any kid of yours yet to be distilled;
deep clean a test-tube, put measures in place;
edit that treasure (white stuff he's *self-killed*).
In olden days such use was usury;
now it happies us to pay-off Nature's loan;
choose responsibly from bestest of thee
lest genius odds equal thousand to one.
Soon all sprogs will conquer math, sports and art,
so no time-wasters, demand alpha thee:
mediocrity's what we must depart
for our genes' journey to posterity.
  Does this sound self-willed? DUH! life's unfair.
  Organic's good for worms, just not my heir.

**R7**

Some prefer to do it by cell phone light
(but get the right contract for your third eye);
pay young porn stars to writhe across their sight
to harden their flagging, er, *majesty*.
But wait! You've beat matrimony's steep hill;
surpassed endowments with middle age;
kept that same, duteous nag waiting still
for luxe cruising–smug retireds' pilgrimage.
Flog it! life's middle crisis Top Gear car,
Bargain Hunt that Four in a Bed today;
don't tell the cash poor kidults where you are -
gift them chez vous–it's the mum'n'dad way:

    Countdown is Pointless—repeat High Noon(!);
    Everybody Loves*...A Place in the Sun.

*Raymond- US sitcom where intimacy issues of married couples
often take centre stage.

## R8

Twitter's tough on spinster divas, sadly
streamed tunes don't translate into spouseal joy;
sweet songbirds penning sick songs will gladly
mug off, call out b'friend's (how they annoy).
Chicks aspire to live off recorded sounds,
Taylor will fight tracks streaming free to ear,
yet she plays a soft porn script that confounds
thinking popstrels—how much should they bare??
Queen Bey stuck it to Jay Z (her other),
but is that real feminist ordering?
Narrative is he's bad, she's a mother;
 solo: how could her notes so sweetly sing?
    Once reconciled *Jayonce* sings as one:
    how duets prove singletons less than none.

## R9

Selfies making love to a dark net's eye
where we indulge in safe, virtual sex life;
the internet, never forget, can't die
(unlike marriage), world wide web's all our wife.
To have, to hold—our vows make me weep;
for richer, for poorer's way WAY behind
paid content addictions we love to keep.
Hun, monogamy is in all our mind.
Look what an unthrift in this world can spend
cash on—banter and harmless porn—spend it!
Libido's gone global, bellend to end,
The Joy of Sex with a cute AI it!
    (O what love for spouses in our bosom sits
    if hyperlinked to what our eye commits?)

## R10

...but do pop some kids out before any
third parties leave your love improvident:
a few too anniversaries too many...
....and you probs won't get what's self-evident.
That's when guys seem more open to wife hate:
they think love's all one big lady conspire...
So you'll take the kids; let him ruinate
X-mas with brand new non-you desire;
watch him run to her in stockings; not mind
for the kid's sake... cos they're the point of love.
Santa–please fill my stocking (not her kind—
tho' what does being a wife or mum prove?)

> Make me some other self, for love of me.
> P.S. No retro—no merry old thee.

## R11

It's our right to freeze lovely us to grow'st;
in case we die, become dear departest;
and that fresh bit which youngly we bestow'st
will outdo death, and brief youth convertest.
Hysterics cry Earth won't cope with increase
that comes from breeding faster that decay:
famines will make us stop, refrain, decease...
any volunteers just to go away?
Make those who can't pay Ms. Nature for store
(cash is her natural selection)- perish!
Buy your brave new world or it's you no more -
what's left is for oligarchs to cherish.

    Huzzah! It's rich perennials left thereby,
    and undeserving poor who rightly die!

## R12

Three score plus ten's not much earthly time
for a barons spicing up the night
with 24/7 news, scripting prime
hypocrite exposees in black, and white.
Shareholders dissent, but nobody leaves;
tax havens safeguard his corporate herd;
off-shore's for ring-fencing assets and sheaves
of cash. Long live that gristly Aussie beard.
Now he's got Big Jerry I think she'll make
him last forever—he's too big to go
tits up like News of the World, for fu**'s sake:
his most trusty bit's frozen to re-grow;

    'gainst Rupe's scythe there's no-one has good
    defence:
    GOTCHA!* (Press freedom can kiss his arse
    hence).

*The Sun newspaper roared into dominance of the UK tabloid
market during the Falkands War (1982), it's patriotic profits
providing the cornerstone for Mr. Murdoch's media empire.
Gotcha! was The Sun's headline when the General Belgrano, an
Argentine cruiser, was sunk.

## R13

O that we were happy with who you are,
ball skills buying gated gaffs where you live;
but pal: us your WAGs suggest you prepare
to share prize DNA that's yours to give.
You'll be our super-car on short term lease
at life's Gumball stud rally (as it were)—
first past the chequered flag of no decease.
You.2's who're we're committed to bear:
showing off the kids will slow your decay—
selfie trophies for players to uphold;
life's not two halves. At the end of the day,
man, when you're hot you're hot; when not, blood's
cold.
    *Nothing*—Anglo Saxon for cunt, you know?
    *Nothings* and football top life and death*, so....?

*"Some people believe football is a matter of life and death, I am very
disappointed with that attitude. I can assure you it is much, much
more important than that."* Bill Shankly

## R14

Earth tilting called out astrology*—pluck
your fate from some star's air?! (Astronomy
is science, therefore not to do with luck
or much loved Russell Grant's star quality.)
Hey our sign's still divine, and so we tell
us sweetly at night, ignoring wind
round the celestial bed (ah well,
your are my genuine shabby-chic find)
under the duvet we choose to derive
much optimism from zodiac art:
so what if only half of cohabs thrive?
Turn that frown upside down! Our stars convert,
    (sciencey boffins might prognosticate)
    compatibility's set at birth-date!

*eg caring Cancer is now a two-faced Gemini.

## R15

Skinny medics groan *How mum's belly grows!*
Midwives shout *Breathe!* every fu★★ing moment;
while I'm scared I presenteth naught but shows
bad genes (mine or dad's? That's some *no* comment);
now they're clocking my milk bar's mass increase:
C to GGG! And blood pressure's sky
high; doc says he'll induce 'fore we decease—
a daughter's born to emperor's memory
LOLZ they cut her out of me. Hope she'll stay
just like me (but with half time four eyes sight)
jinxing Jock's curse (deep dental decay);
and no bastardising bards every night!
　　(Here Will riffed on *youth* minus *th* leaves *you* -
　　Ladies *and* Laddies Macduff- there's your new.★)

★People born as men who receive a womb transplant would
have to give birth by caesarean, medical experts say.

## R16

...consumers find true love the online way
(tho' Virgins Only might be grooming); time
*fugits*, singleton status means decay
(marry yourself for St. Valentine's rhyme!)
Hooked up on Skype all the happy hours
wreaks weakly set privates' settings unset;
*nothings* don't smell sweet like sweet virtual flowers-
it's what's real that stinks like a counterfeit.
Aw! Surfing's put your hard-drive past repair?
Time's past for commuting cursor to pen!
(Guys, if you nurse your limp erm mice, it's fair
ladies make love to plastic rabbits, men.)
    Play with yourself! (Quite old skool, still,
    you've got to love love drawn by handheld skill.)

## R17

Us boomers panting for lattes to come,
feasting off released equity desserts:
Costas' the home from home (not living tomb)
for spending grey pounds, our most vital parts.
Come noon toddlers arrive, affronting eyes:
yum mums don't enforce coffee shop graces.
We love our unpaid child rearing (all lies,
true sentiment's expressed on our faces:
we've been there, done the sick stained t-shirt age,
same old same old rhymes tripping off the tongue.
No Norland nanny could soothe this senior rage:
smack* them in time to that cbeebie's song!)
    Suck on it—we cashed our pots in on time
    (funny how rude and second childhood rhyme).

*Soon to be criminal (in Scotland).

**R18**

Lovers rock up all Summer Of Love day;
on The Big Day cohabs act more temperate -
rough winds do shake the darling buds of May,
saving cash, once that facebook's *saved the date*.
La la ooo tandem honeymoon; sun shines
but *liberté*, *égalité* get dimmed:
*fraternité* saddled *à deux* declines.
Lycra shorts? Please leave landing strip untrimmed.
Those matching tats you got will shortly fade,
(roses on four buttocks get gamely ow'st
between two) romance turns such deathly shade
you're seeking more *me* time and screentime grow'st...

    Lol! *The Dress* is at a thousand likes- see?
    *#foevaaaaa#ilovethee*

## R19

Hot guys stop me to stroke my puppy's paws,
why not? He's cuter than your human brood;
popped out eyes, squashed up snout with useless jaws:
this is two grand of pedigree dug blood.
He can't run away, he's not the fleet'st,
I pull him close to heel at walkies time;
he's an investment–please don't give him sweets
or suggest selective breeding's a crime.
Sad! He's dead! Cheer up! That dear furrow'd brow
gets quickly replaced (for cash) from the pen;
only do-gooders can't dare to allow
that inbreeds bring harmless pleasure to men.
    He's called Dorian* and the name's not wrong:
    his face is fu**ed, but that makes me look young.

*"How sad it is! I shall grow old and horrible and dreadful."
Oscar Wilde, *The Picture of Dorian Gray* (1890)

**R20**

Chelsea M—heroine, traitor painted
up for war on censorship of passion:
East meets West, rogue and straight states acquainted
with cyber tactics, always in fashion;
blowing whistles gets the ole' boys rolling:
big men who come, but not to let peeps gazeth
on secrets dirty oil is controlling
with boy toys that shock, awe, or amazeth.
Fems say God stole Eve's rib when she created
nasty, brutish man kinds no-one's doting
now locker-room bantz sounds limp, defeated:
could scanty sperm counts* breed The Male *Nothing*?
    Germaine says men don't know woman pleasure:
    *wait for it*, Guys!–you'll shrink to girl *treasure*.

*NB Four P's lowering global testosterone:- Plastics,
Preservatives, Produce and Pesticides.

## R21

Marianne's due some credit as *The Stone's* muse;
*Sister Morphine's* less than half Jagger's verse,
and *Sympathy for The Devil* would use
Bulgakov lines she brought him to rehearse.
Slut shaming—long time fem control; compare
she artistes with Sir Mick and other gems;
chanteuses swerving our censure were rare:
even Tammy had to sew her man's hems...*
There's ladies hide with initials to write
(I like a good P. D. James to be fair);
being undisclosed's probably more bright,
such rapey trollsters soil our online air.

    Let them say more that like of hearsay well,
      when femmes don't *put out*... there's nothing to sell.

*Wynette. See *Mike Judge Presents: Tales from the Tour Bus*, Cinemax.

## R22

Bitchhhhh! neck that voddy once you've gone too old
for date night–then you can role play *first date*;
couple of shots down and yaaaaaay let's behold
Channing's Magic Mike, which should expiate
long nights in the sack of he boring thee
and wipe all seedy raiments off your heart:
shout out for the Mrs! RiRi's so me
tats, tats, glorious tats!* Sick grimeish art.
(Uh oh tanked the bottle. She gets wary,
another lovestab ends in tears... O Will
they've gone full Hyde; nasty, mean and chary:
binge boozin' does couples' karma such ill;
    they assume love's dying. It does look slain...
    still breathing...just feeling our age again.)

*An allusion to *The Hearts Song*, written by Hector Nicol, a
St.Mirren fan.

**R23**

Shhhhh to touch your transcendental stage
ladies write-out all stiff leading men part
that's *Us The Movie*; redact rapper's rage
whose strength's abundance weakens every heart.
Man fantasies snake in straight lines (shrinks say),
running commentary's a male psyche rite;
guys swear rude repetitions don't decay
birds enjoyment of the act... baaaabe, it might.
More boudoir silence would be eloquence;
hooters; tits; paps; norks; funbags, all best breast;
but dirty calling them's no recompense
for tendernesses Dick leaves unexpressed.

    Read what dear, Dear Deirdre Sanders* hath writ
    large in photo casebooks- turn down the *shhhh*it.

*Scholars credit John Dunton with initiating the advice column
format in *The Athenian Mercury* in 1691. *"...we refer you to the order
of their* (the sins) *setting down in the Ten Commandments, where
duty to parents is pressed before adultery is forbid."*

## R24

I totes heart you Ryan Reynolds—buff steel'd
torso in my Metro today; I heart
your heart and frame wherein it is held;
I'll take all you home, you fit bit of art.
(Too true that much of you's air-brusher's skill;
and while we're at it, hun, rom coms are lies!
Frankly, my dear, I don't give a damn, still
want to drown in your puppy soft eyes.
I'll *get a room*, let's us be loved-up, done
in with missionary from you to me;
there's windows in my breast through which you,
son,
have Access All Areas. I heart thee.

    Cunning little tweenies don't know what's art—
    dream on Beliebers, Ry is all man heart.

**R25**

Love as per tabloids and zodiac stars
died a death; or so us drunk cougars boast
while grinding on young gentlemen in bars,
reinventing joys we used to fear most...
Styling ourselves on a Heff* centre spread
his *How To* appeal to the third male eye
(star gazey eyes make pride deep buri'ed;
and that Weinstein frown! Brodie's prime might die!)
Divorce is a spent force: net married worth
something J. Rees-Mogg won't ever see foil'ed,
(tho' Jocks do DIY better) is quite
in line with webcam views and threesomes toil'ed.
    Ladies and gents who once were so beloved
    can't remove if their Legal Aid's removed.

*RIP

**R26**

I plead, M'lud, to wedded vassalage;
it's duties left my brow this strongly knit;
his defensive writs, his cheap embassage*,
mere record of insult he claims were wit.
I forget which vintage vinyls are mine,
no pre-nups back in the day to show it;
then we promised mine is yours, all mine's thine:
Love loves a contract, now I think on it.
Whatever. Stars that guide Love are moving
to singular from the mutual aspect,
my last lunar cycle did for loving
what *low fertility* does for respect.
    He's counterclaimed I'm like, psycho bitch *thee*—
    GET OVER IT this is menopause'd me.

*Formal, written message with chivalric associations.

**R27**


In olden time peeps went to sleep in bed;
now it's wasting time just to lie there tired;
ho's* tip tap lit phablets wired to their head
tendering Tinder 'til most lust's expired.
Screens don't honour bedtime or abide
by eight hour shut-eye rule, we're stalking thee
all our small hours, with eyes six inches wide.
*Grrrr!* pics went snail mail for lovers to see
in simpler days; porn stuff hid out of sight;
now our screen's papered with your frontal view -
it's your crown jewels hung in ghastly night
loading... loading... how long can you be new?
 *Love is*...kept alive with a backlit mind;
 and if we sleep, what love is left to find?


*offensive*, woman

**R28**

…get back online, biiiitch!* End this minute's plight,
put our relationship demons to rest,
stay Snapchatting hotly for a *dope* night,
promise not to make you feel (too) oppressed.
Our sun and other planets yet to reign
resend white noise round and round the sky. Me,
I'm on contract minutes and will complain
if dark matter messes me throating thee.
Whaaaaat your ex is texting, for real! She's bright,
and cleavages like that conquer all heav'n;
sooooo broke that you and her hooked up last night -
what happened to *exclusive*, yester even?

    Another quaint habit with us no longer,
      now ladies or bitches are grown stronger.


*Most versatile word in the English language.

## R29

Poor Nigella's papped sans her batwing eyes
(the money shot's stars in a *cast out* state,
shapeless top teamed with jeggings) while she cries,
Cath Kidston bitches devour her just fate.
Burb wives don't do woke existential hope,
just Socratic discourse re men possessed
of bonuses; for her their pity's scope
is small–she's a squilionairesse! at least.
Fem columnists tweet how they're despising
maintenance of the patriarchal state;
how the Daily Mail stops fems arising,
feeds the bitch in us behind our semi's gate...
    So? Enjoy! Pure capitalism brings
      domestic goddesses stuffing broke kings.

## R30

#*midwifecrisis?* Try Mumsnet thought -
how online sisters share their recent past.
Millennials now don't want what you sought,
now they've guessed it's less *Cats*★, more land of waste.
Why didn't you lean in to fight the flow
of bedtime bathes, night after dateless night?
Ergo you're the one to blame for their woe:
making CEO? Ha! well out of sight.
They're in the workplace 'til death's a foregone;
triple locked index linked pensions so o'er;
home reared kids are rare, a luxury move
that was dirt poor, or declassy before.

    That wife/mother/whore thing's your old, rich,
    friend;
     it's zero part hours down you young thing's end.

★*Old Possum's Book of Practical Cats* (1939) A collection of whimsical poems by T. S. Eliot about feline psychology and sociology.

## R31

Thy bosom is endeared with the hearts
of men, old boyfriends; each to each we're dead;
I'm hoping they're ok in all their parts,
pre-texting days is where we're buried.
Years, it's been years since that thought brought a tear
stealing from heart's memory to mine eye;
we give and give and give, we disappear,
 to appear someone else, where dreamings lie.
Not the grave where my buried loves do live,
you're a tree in the park with leaves soon gone
absorbing what last, late summer will give;
 as the leaves fall, every tree stands alone.
    Colours of all I loved I view in thee;
    deepening in you, all fading in me.

**R32**

Here come the hens to Paris for a day,
toting girl porn with hunks on the cover;
there's a stag on board they'll grab to survey:
their traditional mile high club lover.
The crew's having none (still on state side time);
team leader Kate marks our hen seats in pen;
grabs the mic to chide, to shame them in rhyme,
not! Drunk and women—what's not to like, men?
What goes on mid-air, stays mid...hold that thought.
Up the flight deck loo, the queue's an age,
it's where intoxicated hens get brought
for humping dry booze trolleys (equipage*).
    Sent home, they're arrested airside, and prove
    naughty birds *Guilty* of in-flight *um* love.

*Equipment for a *particular* purpose.

## R33

Long and short hauls belch CO2 unseen,
punching holes in your blue atmosphere's eye;
also killing corals as broiling green
seas leak photosynthesised alchemy.
Deny-ers claim there's no proof you won't ride
out fatbergs and flooding… It's not my face
peeling in penance, even while men hide
(yaaay SPF 90!) truth like disgrace.
Helooooo! Helios, god for sunshine
here, flooding you out while I peel your brow.
You need to farm that dead red mate of mine,
make shortish earth years left to you count NOW.
    (Helianthus* will deffo disdaineth
    life on Mars once here's too badly staineth).


*Sunflower genus.

## R34

Why do you spend all the beauteous day
in holing Anthropocene's magic cloak,
thus blowing cosmic cover? Btw
that's not coffee smells got you woke, that's smoke
coming from Das Kapital's collapse, break
down of commodities, no smiley face.
You can hold your nose, but you have to speak
to climate inequality's disgrace.
Guys! You had the science to outwit grief,
then made value judgement a profit/loss;
suspect First to Third World tax relief
off-set against notional *creatures* lost.
    What lives small stars shed (Will, what is this
    *sheeds?*)
    they're all the same to me\*, man's dirty deeds.

\**What has been will be again, what has been done will be done again,*
*there is nothing new under the sun,* Ecclesiastes 1:9.

**R35**

She's got a list for life!* Stuff that needs done:
she'll get her Zen down the spa caked in mud;
she'll get lashes, lacquers and spray on sun -
she'll have a few sessions with Doctor Bud,
she needs to find her G-spot (shrinks spot this);
she could be a bitch, but that's no compare
(she will think) to stuff he did that's amiss.
She'll start living life like we were, not are;
she'll Tinder with toy-boys without much sense,
she's not adverse to what they might advocate;
she's got tools if self-doubts, regrets, commence;
she's steaming her chakras: hating on hate.
     She minus he—can't it feel sss*shit* to be?
     Where's other half, stripped teaser, goddess Me?

*Lust for Life,* song about heroin by Iggy Pop (released 1977).
The lyrics reference William S. Burroughs' experimental novel
*The Ticket That Exploded*, notably "Johnny Yen"- The Boy-Girl
Other Half strip tease God of sexual frustration. (Although
David Bowie wrote the music, on a ukulele.)

**R36**

When's the karaoke?? Shania Twain
knows how to emote two dropping to one
minus; when big cat ladies must remain
game not to live on their pensions alone
sinking voddys. Aretha spells R E S P E C T,
belting out song brings divorcee respite;
bit more voddy for the Tammy effect,
such D.I.V.O.R.C.E.'s delight.
Mahalia! *Just a Closer Walk with Thee!*
I've sung that one ten times o'er without shame:
a touch of the biblicals comforts me
once I'm drunk enough to forget my name.
    (He'll be listening to guys, the angry sort
    like Ike, when Tina got him on report.)

**R37**

Embittered wives- make an effort. Delight
at your estrange'd chasing skirted youth;
it's not about you, the mindset's not spite:
take much comfort from him living his truth.
O how he laughs at her dear, unspoilt wit,
his pals hosing family saloons, and more.
Love's got him by the bollocks, dear: he'll sit,
and beg to obey what lust has in store.
Outworn married sex left yourselves despised
inside: you know you've both got more to give;
big girls and boys accept when love's sufficed
(tho' can't afford separate places to live).

    Look, best is best for both, both he and thee;
    repeat 'til true: *We're ten times happy me.*

**R38**


Carole*, in the Brill building, would invent
ten tunes a day and be paid by the verse;
her musings on love still sound excellent—
*Will You Still Love Me?* sick girl bands rehearse.
Girl Power empowered us to be tonnes more me
as nine old muses shuffled out our sight.
It's so not dumb–I, me's my mostest thee
since we invented sex and eco light:
bloke tunes are sounding outworn of their worth.
Oh! Carol* where's the heav'n you invocate,
where swans married from initial first kiss forth
(so it is ok to do sex first date?)?

> We're all our own, our own slight muse these days:
> writing hackney tunes, singing cliché praise.


*Carole King. Neil Sedaka (*Oh! Carol*) went out with her in High
School- when she spelt her name without the "e".

**R39**

What goes on the road stays on the road sing
troubadours: all of us, it seems to me—
who will their own praise to their own self bring;
and what is it but our own when we praise *thee?*
And it's like this boomers divided live,
*Us* in only name; both glad singles, one
from Venus, one Mars or both, who won't give
in, compromise. They want.....to be alone.
In separate cities these estrangers prove
their own best critics—too late now to leave
that concept album they've been writing: love
players, long players with words that deceive
　　them no longer; they will not live as twain
　　but two ones apart. *Love is*★... to remain?

★A single frame comic strip started in the 1960s originating from
a series of love notes its creator (Kim Casali) drew for her future
husband. At the height of their popularity in the 1970s they
earned her £4-5 million annually (!).

**R40**

Hotties barely rate chuffies*, if at all;
*no oil fu**ing painting*- heard that before.
Life is a chick flick and cruel casting call
when you're five out of ten. Would I was more.
But....should cute Reese Witherspoon receivest
my part, there's free rein for her to usest
me the mostest: I won't you deceivest -
if Hollywood calls–who should refusest?
I forgive you already LA thief;
relieve my shortish *friend* list poverty,
despite global social media grief
because Reese is the twin of me. What injury
    a mega grossing bio pic that shows
    me down with starry ho's and other foes?

*fat-faced people

## R41

It's not adultery if your head commits
it, that way shame's absented from your heart;
every advance in robot sex befits
us, given that a good VR's their art.
Gentle we were, and therefore to be won:
since the gloves came off, we're all assailed,
aggro *lite* love so betters every son
and it, so plasticity has prevailed.
Married for E-V-A-H. Your seats won't forbear
you and your missus from not buying youth;
the dream of guilt-free sex was always there,
watch *Metropolis*⋆ if you want the truth.

    We'll get one each (it's not good sharing *thee*,
    but make sure your bot's the double of me).

⋆1927 sci-fi with lots of biblical references! Freder (main protagonist) imagines false Maria, anti-heroine robot, as The Whore of Babylon at one point.

**R42**

...you've switched me for her?? she'll bring you bot grief,

get ready to regret your move dearly;

she'll have you by your lady curlies chief—

you'll want back my small treasure then nearly...

She yells lout stuff like *How do I love Ye?*

I did my level best to reboot her,

it was unnerving how she fixed on me,

so I had to keep flicking *Off* on her

(same sex with a robot brought me no gain).

When you switch her her back *On*, expect some loss

of power, it's pointless to be kind: retrain

her to bear domesticity's dull cross,*

    thus should we all reward our chosen one:

    *not only men do that to dames alone.

**R43**

On the Facebook again–what those eyes see
young moderators call unrespected.
He says he's not trying to sextort thee,
that knee jerk censorship's misdirected;
non consensual intimacy's not bright;
there's a hot key to disable such show;
plus image matching software to make light
work of tsunamis of revenge porn, so
why not simulate anon sex jests made?
Why not celebrate cyber freedom day?
Hard relationships belong in the shade,
backlit eyes where our real virtual dreams stay.
    All nights are days of fetishzising thee
    when I can see you, but you can't touch me.

## R44

Living's mere existing without *some* thought,
go to guru's show life's cerebral way;
reason why is it time and space have brought
uncensored stuff to places where we stay.
If their intellectualising won't stand,
let's all play *eeny meeny miney* thee
or spin a bottle to see if we land
on what we think nice behaviour should be.
On the other hand, do you think that thought
might swamp us when all finer feeling's gone?
Or voyeurism leave us overwrought,
when we attend leisure time with our moan?
　　What to do with bodies defunct and slow
　　but return them to their elements. Wow! (or Woe!)

**R45**

My granny liked to throw them on the fire,
hard copies of peeps she couldn't abide;
Wim★ says snaps now don't rouse hate or desire—
it's show and send—memory's on the slide.
You hit *delete* hun to make me be gone:
lol who's your lockscreen if I'm dead to thee?
With a phone we must never be alone,
ghosting's murder by our melancholie.
I might buy an app to get me recured
of bad vibery and hating on thee;
what you give comes round again, be assured
of this thing–I've wiped your dick pics to me.
    Unsolicited (did they make me glad?)
    aye, there's the bummer- they're gone, and I'm sad.

★Wenders

**R46**

Your eye and heart are at some mortal war
with rude Tinderistas in moby's sight;
the jury says to hit the singles bar
(they don't find youth on your side, ok? Right.)
What's foregone is that guys scalade* then lie,
while ladies want love mirrored in their eyes
(ladette defendants might that plea deny):
proof's on your breast, the tattoo never lies.
Let's get your Tinder pals re-empanelled
and rule on lasering him off your heart;
CBT will make you quite determined
tholing pain that's under your nipple part.
    Hun! it's a *Not Proven* if you should part:
    there's a too much scarring over your said heart…

*What Burns did to poor Jean Armour. NB Unlike Carole King
(see *R38*) Burns dropped an *e-* he was born *Burnes*.

**R47**

So, that couple's mediation you took
en route to ex-significant other
identified she owes you a new look
if you stop bitchin' about her sMother.
Neither of you's a bod for eyes to feast
but there's billions of beats left to each heart
that doesn't let vengeful thought be a guest
(colonic flushes don't reach that far part).
How about a unicorn tat to love
(speech bubble reading *All's Magic in Me!*)
like Stubbs' Whistlejacket caught in mid-move?
(He drained horse blood, what's a few pricks to thee?)
    With the horn on you're a mythical sight
    who no unicornesse shouldn't delight.

**R48**

...even Ryan made Joi the Stepford way,
slim simulacrum of desire for his thrust,
a pleasure replicant on short Earth stay....
come 2049–who will we trust?
Meanwhile us negotiating love are
too cash poor to live separately less grief;
worth funner lifetimes, we'll show how we care,
won't be each other's life ambition thief:
take a catalogue. Let him choose her chest
(prepare yourself for stereotypes as art);
NuWives4U gives us all a clean breast
at menages a trois missing out euuuuwww part.
 She's insurable 'gainst fire, flood and fear
 that in such events–it's her you'd save, dear.

## R49

Against that hour (dear heart, I think it's come,
see *The War of the Roses*★), when defects
we count in each of us equals a sum
off the Brexit debt scale in it's respects.
Against that hour when the dog's had to pass
(I'll feel large bits of me die in her eye)
let's us recalibrate our love as was,
pre-Isaac falling foul of gravity.
Against that hour not one of us lives here
and the garden's resorted to desert;
let's make civilised memories to uprear;
let's do lunch, mwah mwah the air when we part,
    proving most profitable of all laws:
    how divorce beats nostalgia, our lost cause.

★1989 *When a wealthy couple's seemingly perfect marriage falls apart,
they descend into ever more shocking and outrageous behaviour over
their shared possessions.*

**R50**

*Just Passed!* she drivers want it all their way,
don't mess with the lurid Barbie wheels, end
of. Lane discipline—lame advice! Say
it and you're the frenemy not her friend.
An ice queen cometh steering 4 x wheel woe,
bearing down on lowly drivers like me;
who's voicing up her sat nav I don't know:
it doesn't involve giving way to thee.
I might pimp my ride, a panic room on
wheels en route supermarkets where I'll hide
in the car park for a wee cry and groan:
so often the sisterhood's not on side.
    Basics of feminism come to mind.
    Who's *not for turning*, what's *The Power*\* behind?

\*by Naomi Alderman - Winner of the 2017 Baileys Women's
Prize for Fiction (NOT Baileys Prize for Women's Fiction).

## R51

*Hungover Parent On Board!* No offence
if you stick to small distance at low speed
round and round domestic tracks thence and thence:
come bedtime—houghmagandy*? There's no need:
severe dairy, er, bloating works we find,
damping urges when um steerage feels slow.
Still chancing it, despite the threat of wind?
Scunnert** at starter's orders, old wives know
we're not favourites in this panto horse pace
well stuck in the arse end Kirstie's*** hand made:
silly moos- lost our head before the race,
now fresh fillies ride your old dear, dear jade...

    Double the HRT–stupid is slow
    when Poundland's selling sex toys. Get set... go!

*Colourful Scots language: i)fornication (obsolete, except as a
reminiscence of Burns, etc.) ii) a feeling of aversion, disgust, or
loathing.
*** Allsop

**R52**

Most days I'm fantasising fame's the key
to free couture, that A-Lister treasure:
my kid needs Hermes bags to survey
mixed in with *giving something back* pleasure.*
Therefore is my sense crazy, also rare,
obvs I'm closer to life in the Z set.
How much cash is where *so called* celebs are?
That's the captain jewel in life's carcanet.
(Constant recognition's bad for the chest,
heads shoved under airless blankets to hide
post nights with just a mate who's been blessed...
Helloooo! Privacy's dead, so is pride.)
    Blessed are poor civvies for they have scope
    to live earthy lives anon. We don't hope.

*See *Tamara's World* on ITVBe, or catch up on the ITV Hub.
Tamara (nee Ecclestone) spent £70,000 on her daughter's first
birthday party.

**R53**

Whither your substance Kim*, of what are you made
that billions of followers on you tend,
since every one has, everyone, one shade**-
but you, with one, can every shadow lend?
Describe me Miss World and the counterfeit
is poorly imitated after you;
on your bottom cheeks all art of beauty set;
then you broke the internet -wow that's new.
Speak of the Spring, also Rear of the Year,
the first but shadows of your beauty show,
the other as your award doth appear
(plus you by every pubic inch we know).
    In all selfie graces you have some part,
      but you like none, none you, for selfie heart.

*Kardashian

**Image

## R54

Scripted teen reality stars who seem
to have more self to throwaway than give;
their addictions, their dependencies we deem
collateral damage for the way they live.
Year long they bloom with skins of tattooed dye
—unicorns and buttocks full of roses—
you've got to love them as they wantonly
emote crap scoops this week's prog discloses.
Where's those idols silver screens used to show?
CHANEL made Marilyn M. shrink and fade
(skeletal starlets wear No 5, so
it seems curvy dames can't up sell what's made).
    Kids, kids, you're selling your self with youth.
    When that shall vade*—what of you smells like
    truth?

*go away, Latin *vadere*

## R55

Vicky gave her Bert his own monuments
(prince among men he loved high art and rhyme)
I beg to address within these contents
how those stones survive rain and sluttish time?
What if us subjects voted to o'er turn
that £10m worth of masonry
(who's worth that now if we had cash to burn?)
revealing what props up Bert's memory
'gainst subsidence and other enmity?
Clue; he's held aloft a navvy bricked room
hid from loyal plebs for posterity
to keep his end up, 'til Team GB's doom!
    Rise me old cock (ring) Prince Albert, arise!
    God save all stately secrets from our eyes!

**R56**


Watched Wilde last night–loads of what Oscar said
riffed on Shakespeare—gross sexual appetite;
Bosie's* mad sex drive not getting allayed;
an artist's pen stronger than his *um* might.
Steve Fry was good, he got the screen to fill
with the platonic (or Greek) ideal of fullness;
Jude Law–gorge; wee Martin Sheen got first kill;
Jennifer Ehle shone with a wife's sad dullness.
Still, I didn't expect how tearful I'd be
(they're always repeating it, it's not new)
by shots of her grave...I mean, what's to see?
The Buggery Act's** a long repeal'ed view...

    (The Mail will weigh genius by duty of care;
    hypocrisy's maybe still not that rare.)


*Lord Alfred Douglas
**The Buggery Act 1553, formerly *An Acte for the punishment of the vice of buggerie.*

## R57

I read wives of bigamous husbands tend
to internalise what they don't desire
to detect from his last MasterCard spend,
avoiding what action truth may require...
She bins his tea—it's been cold for an hour—
texts him See *dog for what was meant for you*;
dwelling on his absence feels like sour,
who's not bid fear of the cheater *adieu*?
(Not sure I'd know what to do with the thought
mine might have more than one missus... suppose
I did walk–would it all have been for nought?
Years of denial–you don't get back those.)
    So love makes us fools then fools our free will?
    (Heads-up! Game's a bogey if he gets ill...)

**R58**

Pure self-indulgent whining *I'm his slave!*
(I could with thought control my urge for pleasure)
but a live-in maid's what millions of us crave
for ring-fencing time to max out on leisure.
We want a willing pinny at our beck
(no to health safety checks or liberty);
these gymbods need kept in bitchtastic check,
why risk housework related injury?
My rationale for paid help's super strong,
us household execs. prioritise time:
workouts and poolside are where we belong;
*let herself go-* worstest modern crime!
    A life less lived–not going to be my hell.
    Life's unfair, but what can you do? Ah well.

**R59**


Nothing new under the sun, that which is,
gets old–but Nokia's got me beguiled
with all things lo-tech: who knew we'd miss
nineties brick handsets built for a child?
Take a scroll down then, a long backwards look
to a kinder, cooler, less UV sun;
pre-free porn net usurping every book,
and showing under 5's how sex is done.
Outsize buttons keep it simple to say
*I love you* in a square vintage style frame;
but textings it's sending from me to they
look graphic—maybe love's just not the same?
    MC Leonard Sachs on *The Good Old Days**
    wears period dress, shouts period praise.


*Chic Murray joke from The Good Old Days: *If it wasn't for marriage, husbands and wives would have to fight with strangers.*

**R60**

Birds on the game wave from 50+ shore,
we seniors who'd hoped for respectful end;
transpires we have to die quickly before
butchered pensions are all WASPI'S* contend;
*nothings* are our equity, slits of light;
Liz, *ER I*, the virgin queen as crowned,
beheaded her cousin—what a cat fight!
So let us male-hearted cougars confound
theft of contributions made in our youth;
no dead lead foundation but Botox'd brow;
young men seem to prefer us, in all truth,
altho' the lady garden's scant to mow**.

    Byee! chaste life from bare shores where we stand;
    tide's rolling in on the State's helping hand.

*Women Against State Pension Inequality
**Or... *It vexed me sair, It put me in a passion, To think that I haed wad a wife, Whase cunt was oot o' fashion.* See *Nae Hair On'*tby Robert Burns.

## R61

*Get Snapchatting* crankous* chakras open!
Us playas don't want REM at night,
but waaaay uncool if slumber is broken
with pics of him bangin' babes in your sight.
This deus ex my machina is thee,
out the house, yet under sheets you pry,
demanding three-ways (you, a her and me)
what feasts technology feeds jealousy!
Oh no, your sight though much, is not so great;
I will diarise this, now I'm awake:
note to self- hooking up online- DEFEAT;
and stop thumbing thru' Thrinder** ffs***!
    Still struggling to block sexploits from elsewhere?
    Howk out social apps showing them so near.

*fretting, peevish
**Forced to change its name to *Feeld* after a nasty copyright dispute with *Tinder*.
***for f**k sake

## R62

The class tutor claims I have a good eye
sketching my hairy hips, ladyee fair part;
she says self-portraiture's good remedy
when the angst of ageing hits your heart.
Methinks no face so gracious is as mine,
no shape so true, no truth of such account
as these vital XL stats I define,
(good luck with that, that bitch fat to surmount,
bitch!) then my glass showed me, the self. Indeed...
I'll pay tanned guys not of antiquity
to model: much much more pleasure to read...
(Poor Generation Rent's iniquity:
> zero hours that's paid in cash or er praise,
> while rich old *limmers** draw their younger days.)

*Women of easy virtue; often confused with *limners*: painters of
ornamental decoration.

**R63**


Don't you rubbish this look I sport now!
Birthwork, housework, more work, left me o'er
worn:
also necking wine 'til sofa meets brow,
then clutching Costas' into work next morn.
Mid-afternoon I'm deep in steepy night:
gimme gimme gimme caffeine size King:
once youth's elastane starts dropping from sight
naff decaff won't resurrect that short Spring!
Discreet clinics offer to fortify
without recourse to private surgeon's knife;
wipe that wasted face from your memory
(with a tidy-up once a year for life).
  Cheers m'dears to years of me being seen
  com *vinho verde*, but not young, not green.

**R64**

...stop saying I'm by time's fell hand defaced
condemning me to be burial age;
forbye I believe 'fore yon Shard's erased
we'll have an app to kill RIP rage!
Til then... fine that my savings are state gain,
someone needs to pay for the care home shore;
yes, let my corpse be win of the watr'y main,
then recycle me quick for earth's due store...
But Evita* looked lush lying in state,
hurry up! with that app to halt decay:
it should make politicos ruminate
if voters can refuse to rot away?
     Real democracy means die if you choose—
     why should Gaia dictate who we lose?

*Peron

**R65**

Since jobs, nor shifts, nor hours, nor rising sea
outlasts rise of computers' higher power;
how with their rage can workers make their plea,
whose action is no stronger than a flower?
O how can man's mentality hold out
to fight AI siege of his working days
when no white or blue collar is so stout,
nor any union strong, but bot decays?
Bananas share most of our genes, alack;
unless an omnipotent maker hid
a superpower in ours–man's heading back
to his dystopian past, god forbid!
    Season tics for Premier League leisure might
    make losing the job (heard this before?) bright.

**R66**

Tired of all these, for restful death I cry:
as to us beggars good Prince George was born
and payday loan sharks promised jollity,
and a man's a man for a' that forsworn,
and bankers for Liz make off-shores misplaced,
and pageant queens under 5 strumpeted
and mums wearing baby fat are disgraced,
and who's poor by who's not disable'd
and corporates stealing art's authority,
and Si's profit making *X Factor* skill,
and true news confused with complicity,
and cheap sweetmeats making us fat and ill.
    Tired with all these, from these I would be gone,
    or is it just *Grauniad* me alone?

**R67**


Not mementoes mori, cheerful me's live
on my mantelpiece with impunity;
they're 3D tributes printers achieve
for titled and not of society;
I got The Three Graces bum and face cheek
deal–BOG2U's*, love that magenta hue.
Why would I beauty indirectly seek?
Why shouldn't idealised me come true
before my bod with Nature bankrupt is,
in shorts, grossly flaunting varicose veins?
I'll soon pay earth's due debt, give God what's his,
I'm leaving you 3 wee me's–knick knack gains,
    miniatures, mostly what aristos had.
    We're all our own Hilliard**. Good, or bad?


*Buy One Get 2 U's

** Nicholas Hilliard (1547-1619)- miniaturist painter to the Elizabethans.

**R68**

She says my charms for her have gone outworn;
that we need a lot of work on us now;
mean allegations of bar-steward I've borne
stressed my follicles, hence baldness at brow.
Before the golden dreadlocks were all dead,
she suggested I get them shorn away;
gey few rastas are aka jarhead—
why not extensions to make me feel gay?
She's hit *netaporter.com* and seen
real subcontinent stuff (no horse tail). True—
I'm buying summer that's Indian green;
but exploiting The Empire–is that new?
    It's the natural add on for my thin store;
    hairploitation blah blah–yesterday's yore.

**R69**

Tight shots straw PR guys put in our view
plus sound-bites: how you'll get us on the mend
and give hard working families their fair due;
uttering vows even Scot Nats must commend.
Old Trots get their social credentials crowned
when vast Glasto crowds rush to sing; they own
youth's glad vibe... but ballots confound—
like when silent majorities are shown.
Spraffy pollsters don't get the public's mad mind,
gaps appear 'twixt predicted votes and deeds;
now age is proxy for class, so not kind
to let green shoots be strangled by us weeds.
　　I doubt *The People's Flag* is what we'll show
　　when soil is this: us weeds doth common grow.

## R70

Vampire Squid Brothers suffer one defect:
*excess standard deviation*—unfair
play! they say, it's brute Nature we suspect
of killing our algorithms with air
and not lame governments' job to approve
sub prime dodgy loans. George* gave them time
with a quantitative easing type of love:
the economist's snub to sub sub-prime!
In old post industrial declining days
all debt felt small enough to be discharged;
we used to singalonga *Songs of Praise*
(Sir Jimmy's** hits got hushed up, not enlarged).
    I bet you currency's a busted show,
    and I'll raise you bankers spent all we owe.


*Osborne
**Saville OBE (Order of the British Empire), KCSG (Knight Commander of St.Gregory the Great)

**R71**

Central Park luvvies* acted POTUS dead:
The Donald muffled that liberty bell
(Toots*, man!) so dissenting personae fled
from that enclave round which billionaires dwell.
Bank of America's in shock—no not
regarding sub sub-prime mortgages so
much as bit players: the ninnies forgot
to remember Trumpy satire brings woe.
Shut-up! if you declaim in bawdy verse
re dictator properties built on clay,
self-censorship's what you needs must rehearse,
democracy schmockracy's in decay.
     *Fu\** Your Feelings\*\**, you pinko commie moan!
     (And some liberals too want what's left-wing gone.)

---

*New York Times, June 11th 2017- Bank of America's withdrawal of sponsorship from a free production of Julius Caesar in Central Park.

**Seen on t-shirts worn by President Trump supporters.

## R72

Sing, Up wi't! if you want to recite,
muse encore on heteronormative love,
aye but hide from mad Twitter's sphere that quite
eviscerates women who might disprove
all misogyny a bleeding heart lie;
that feminists deserve rape's just dessert;
oh those scatological jokes, jibes—I
am scared of what trolling twitters impart.
Maybe I read too much shite into this,
trolls for love speak things of all men untrue;
my right-wing conspiracy theory is...
they're everywhere! They're after me and you!
    Just by being me, or you, brings hate forth;
     but their hate is not love, and nothing worth.

**R73**


I'm more mim-mou'd* now than loud to behold;
rich old idealists like me don't hang
or chain ourselves to fences in the cold
at Faslane or Greenham, where young birds sang.
I've ended up at twilight of a day
that's seen the death of open house in the West,
our vigils chase migrating birds away,
the global race for jobs affords no rest.
There's my morals in the vanities fire
where the ashes of *red* convictions lie
with experience, where beliefs expire
consumed with fear we've not enough *put by*.
    When we marched in those demos we felt strong;
    who knew know old age would last so long?


*quiet-spoken

## R74

Once this earth holds me back under arrest,
and all my trophies Lord, laid down, away:
I won't care there's hundred per cent interest,
casino banks corrupted this short life's stay.
(Now I want an IFA* to review
if my life policy might fall to thee,
the ex i.e. *No* big payouts your due
if it's got anything to do with me.)
So much for all that then, c'est la vie, life—
a free lunch for worms and a long time dead;
or fodder for the callow medic's knife?
Free gifts to research get remember'ed:
    hope they find out how the genome contains
    the love of money gene in my remains.

*Independent Financial Advisor

**R75**

A stealthy, wealthy elite sort of life
defines estate as in country playground;
and servants to cope with everyday strife
(non-dom gold paves the London streets they found).
Tenants banging on no fire doors anon,
(this filching age has stolen such treasure)
the towers burn–looks like poor folks alone
squandered per square meter. For who's pleasure?
Youth asleep on the street offends my sight,
another generation with no look
in on shareholder windfalls–what delight,
scrounging bens, what a lifestyle choice they took!
    Thus do we stuff and surfeit day by day,
      few gluttoning on those who're soon away.

**R76**

My Sunday supp features LV* heels, pride
of *Made in Italy* craftsmen; they change
what's built in Romania (soles aside)
into deluxe'y designer–quite strange
we don't value two countries work the same;
that would price up a rose same as a weed,
and conflate inherent worth with brand name:
a green light for new Europe to proceed.
If shoes you make take months to earn (for you)
—so what? Living wage, goes the argument
(plus coffee breaks, flushing loos!) is the new
economics. (We get less than we've spent:

    fashion launders capital, as of old,
    and dumb fashionistas wear what they're told.

*Louis Vuitton. A worker in LV's secret Romanian factories
(where the LV *Made in Italy* shoes are actually made) would take
6 months to earn enough to buy a pair of their mid-price courts.

**R77**

Use your phablet to shop my activewear
and fitbit to track muscle mass or waste;
best you can be is what online should bear
—only post your happy bits in good taste;
such bingo wings selfies so cruelly show
are reminders not fit for your memory.
Slapping on a filter (try Need to Know)
means you looking great for eternity,
locks down a likeness where you can contain
it, forever updating til you find
pure synergy of BMI and brain;
guidelines say body matters over mind.
      Here's how to get that must have *After* look:
      read my blog, watch my prog, and buy my book.

**R78**


My fave app is a nihilist social muse
that allows me to ignore other's verse;
it forwards cheesy photos I can use
when I feel the urge to swipe and disperse.
It's plink plink plink noise makes my neurons sing
liking or retweeting by Twitterwing;
I give stock photos double majesty,
spreading what it's algorithms compile:
as such, content untouched by human thee.
It happies me to spread a programme's style:
how human does a hashtag have to be?
　　Am I, I worry, fuelling bot advance,
　　FOMO* thumbing art out of ignorance?


*Fear Of Missing Out- anxiety that an exciting or interesting event may currently be happening elsewhere, often aroused by posts seen on social media.

**R79**


BOGOF *slaves* BOGOF *migrants* BOGOF *aid*
for Thai fishermen who drown to grace
miles of groaning striplit shelves with decayed
crustaceans, clingfilmed in a plastic place.
(We're all we eat's my simple argument,
prawns dye flamingos pink, same thing with men;
yet what madness thy poet doth invent;
she's trying metaphysical, again).
They're thrown overboard on gangmaster's word
or trawl some years for some few dollars–give
up guys or be fish food we afford;
they eat you: we eat them. How not to live.
    *Don't say* Is it sustainable? *Do say*
    Yum, king prawn cocktail–card ok to pay?

**R80**

Macron gets it–press outlets love to write
up men who still give fit ladies their name;
Brigitte's old as Trump is to his wife—might
as well be nought—their currency is fame.
For your vote to ride high as ocean is
deep, your spouse is required to thole, bear
offences of state: his or her's or his;
your public's waiting for cracks to appear.
Stout royal dynasties can keep afloat
manning fillies like boarding craft that ride
toward good ship Modern Monarchy's boat:
a royal wedding rescues national pride.

    Chancellors waved the gold standard away;
    but marriage will save our states from decay!

## R81

You poets, means of production who make
*fal, lal, & co* out emotion, rotten
there's no firewall to save care you take:
and whae's noble in being forgotten?
Flytings, cadged sang o' sangs are all we have
(it's 70 years copyright if you die);
*fal lal's* must appreciate out the grave
to halt an oeuvre's death—the *likes* don't lie;
earth internet's bound to consume verse
which eyes not yet created shall o'er read;
jovial You Tubers sample, rehearse,
digital remains of bards barely dead.
    Lal de dal lal lal all fruits of my pen
    free and freer to be exploited by men.

**R82**

Brummie Bill* goggled London for his muse;
hyper-connectivity lets us look
through global gene pools loveless lovers use:
not just contacts writ in a calfskin book.
Saxon and Celt of peely-wally hue
weren't Easyjetting out for sun praise:
us Elizabethans, breeding anew,
will circle Puck's whole earth for wedding days.
What language should our rulers have devised
that will evolve (fast as our hearts can lend)
unabsurd words to say we've sympathized
when we're hooked up with a new foreign friend?
    Heigh-ho Esperanto? Never been used.
    Lo! Googlese renders us disabused.

*Scholars are divided as to how similar Shakespeare's accent was
to Ozzy Osbourne's.

## R83

To *Bottoms Up!* down Lothian Road: need
refreshment? Lolz the licence got reset
ripped pole dancers' tips failed to exceed
build ups of Universal Credit debt.
I wonder what they thought of this report:
"...not cool now for paying punters to show
hard cash devotion—that's selling you short,
girls' rights must shun currency to grow:
bouncy Jane Austens* in knickers impute
us as mere strippers. Feminism's dumb!
Postgraduate pole dancers aren't mute
while *Pussy Riot's* kicking Stalin's tomb..."
    Hoots, Jocky! *Sex worker* offends my eyes -
    an economic model pimps devise.

*Polymer notes are cleaner and more hygienic because they can
be wiped clean, of anything.

## R84

Truth is the self of you—what can say more
than your own praise, that you alone are you
(selfies proving this live in a clouds' store),
and it's from your self that your best self grew.
Aforesyne nunneries were where to dwell
for long lifetimes of herself-obsessed glory
deffo followed by good afterlife, tell
me who wants to play at bride in that story?
I am my own *habeas corpus** writ
thus making moral entitlement clear;
a neo-liberal self has the wit
to admit that the self is...everywhere!
    We are what we do (Aristotle's curse)
    being fond on praise, making self praise worse.


*Doesn't operate in Scotland, as any fule kno.

**R85**

Philosophers make up conundrums, still
rejecting *.com's* and *Love* got compiled,
and Tinder rules how we feel since the quill
lost to thumbs and deference was misfiled.
With machines to replay all our love words
(first word processors were bibles, *Amen*)
opportunities one moby affords
exceeds all Will's stiff ostrich feather pen…
NASA, *The Sun* says (so I know it's true),
is working on us talking less, not more,
they're sending thoughts from them to me to you,
messages doctors were spinning before.
    Guys! Slow down, show some *ABC* respect.
    Minds at crude hyper-speed mute love effect.

**R86**

Wullie, soz for this, this aping your verse,
dissing bootaaay of all-too-precious you,
and there's yet sixty-seven I could inhearse,
my ego's the *womb to tomb* where they grew.
I've no spirit, Wullie, rags that I write
are killing love's weak sense of mystery dead;
meta data bombs the harn-pan* each night,
making it hard to be astonish'ed.
I would will myself to be but some ghost
writer of worldwide web intelligence;
or able to voice a free gendered boast,
write to live with love, not fear of what's thence…

    Wullie, unknowing you willed ends of line;
    the rest, un*will*int emptiness, is mine.

* brain-pan, skull.

**R87**

Past sell-by for one on one possessing,
monogamish is our best guestimate;
systemic failures of Love are releasing
us from *I do* (too indeterminate).
Step 1 agree what safe sex games you're granting,
by acknowledging all who are deserving
Step 2 don't die undersexed or more wanting;
and nb it's like, swinging more than swerving;
Step 3 why not polyamory? Knowing
me knowing you has meant us fuds mistaking
*Origin of Species* for love; us growing
Jock Tamson's bairns is pure *lifestyle choice* making!
    Multiple partners–the dream that doth flatter.
    And reproduction, that's a small matter.

**R88**

...those who choose to wear sacred vows more light

ly, rightly they're wary of public scorn:

erstwhile swinging partners up for a fight—

it's always the wife's rep that's gets forsworn.

My sexologist, we're well acquainted,

wrote a thousand page bonkbuster story,

on how monogamism's attainted

(compromised) by loving past first glory.

He said I should be more relax'ed too;

stop bending all my sexual thoughts on thee;

the injury that to myself I do

is so beneath this free spirit that's me...

    Mebbes... more like I'm so old I belong

    where *happily married* doesn't sound *wrong.*

**R89**

Idols fear the dark net finds them at fault
buttrust pricey briefs stave off press offence
and intrusion. Super injunctions halt
sex exposers in million pound defence.
Happy throuples, who're doing no-one ill,
down your local swingers club they're small change;
but Hollywood moguls then and now will
suppress what makes their dream machine seem...
strange.
Premier League pricks would silence that tongue
of a print press beast where freedoms still dwell;
and family value MP's who've done wrong
cite due legal process 'gainst kiss'n' tell.

    All wigged up in the courtroom briefs debate
    ways to shaft. And then who, who's not to hate?

**R90**

An' *hey for houghmagandie's* gone, spent now;
we all, all feel wrung out, nailed to the cross
of compromise; it's killing you to bow
all your hours to vows. Let's explore this loss:
post-honeymooning's end to end sorrow,
which made you early adopters of woe;
bedeen!* more yesterday than tomorrow,
*we's* easier to keep than *overthrow*.
If you do leave *us*, don't leave me to last,
when the fouterie griefs have done their spite;
make it 'fore I'm fifty that I might taste
airse end of a one date sex life, or might.

 And these strains of woe, which don't seem woe
 when thereanent** *us*, oh, they will seem so.

*quickly, soon, early. Used here as an expletive to eke out a line
of poetry on marriage.

**in opposition to

## R91

Some glory in their birth, some in their skill,
some in their wealth, some in their pec's rude force,
some in their garments, though slave-fangled ill,
some in their hawks and hounds, some in their horse.
We need to commune re rich peep's pleasure;
where we want folk's mobility to rest:
dismiss *equal's* idealist measure,
posit equal opportunity best.
Brain training's better than high birth to me;
 education education... What cost
is market rate for dreamy spires to be?
Global Elite 1st Class! the shabby boast.
 Unis say how much we pay, who they'll take;
 that's cant. Those choices are for us to make.

**R92**

...say Jockies ditch free uni anyway—
how to future proof the kids, yours and mine?
is there a country left we'd like to stay
where hard currencies don't define all thine?
Is it naive unimagining wrongs?
Since dosh knows no borders, do states end
up being where the biggest vault belongs,
vaults on which no legalities depend?
And social mobility? How to mind
that gap where Left and Right failures lie?
(Remind me to remember not to find
I got given some Ladyship 'fore I die:

    call me snowflake, but I don't want that blot!
    That nobility's mobility *not*...)

## R93

So shall we live (hard to swallow Al's* true,
we're all deceived by his oh so smooth face,
polar caps melting is probs nothing new,
and North Britain's better a hotter place!)
searching those gods who were our weather eye,
the ones in charge of predictable change
and paleo man's climate history.
What saint to call on when rainfall's all strange
despite another G20 decree?
Have faith they'll save us a nice place to dwell!
Our elected heads of (most) states will be
committed ecologists (but don't tell…).
    Sad. Like Eve's apple, my doubts, their lies, grow;
    and green deeds promised honour not earth's
    show.

*Gore

**R94**

Mindfulness minus wellness equals none;
gospel according to gurus who show
us how to drop that sinful extra stone;
be reborne—stop gulping! And chew more slow,
six-packs are to die for hard core graces:
they're the guid lords and maisters of our faces,
our heads but stewards of their excellence;
ask Gwynnie who lives on *Goop!* how she's sweet:
(it involves tanned, toned abs before you die)
pay a squillion* (don't be a bitch) to meet,
honour her outer beautie's dignity.
    Sisters shouldn't diss her by words or deeds:
    fifty quid's cheap for a *Smoothie o' Weeds*.

*Tickets to a one day *In Goop Health* conference cost between
$500 and $1,500.

**R95**

Weans, bairns, while you're unfamous peeps you're shame;
get exposure while you're fresh as a rose;
no-brainer choice for bigging-up your name
to earn that privilege poshos enclose.
Let your bod be the story of your days
(joining a band now's more rarefied sport),
XXL pecs'n'boobs guarantee praise,
*Love Island* orgies for *Metro*\* to report.
O what a mansion have your vices got,
trampled on the bus, gossip pics of thee:
who gets moolah for them? Aye, there's the blot;
caught in stills no-one needs to pay to see.
    That paper's not free of old privilege
      feeding on your youth, dulling your sweet edge.

\*Part of the same media group as *The Mail* and *The Mail on Sunday*.

## R96

Dear Will, Will you forgive my wantonness,
piggybacking on you for shameless sport?
Your grace grows more while my fault grows no less:
I think I despise my wit's last resort!
Ay but as I'm no Miss Scotland gene queen
I'm yaukit* by handsome looks you esteemed
(ok, you knew they let faults hide unseen)
maybe that's my problem with stuff you deemed?
Rabbie B was the same oops! I betray,
but tell me I'm wrong. Male poets translate
what us gazers can't tear our eyes away
from—it's blokey gaze brought us to this state!
    Yours, and soz again writing in this sort,
      sometime I hope for romance to report.


*perplexed, perturbed

## R97

That's a half century now since we've been
gay and glad and proud every time of year;
but don't you think it's weird how fast we've seen
the rainbow hyperbranded everywhere?
Down the British Library–spend some time
'til your train (*love* Dick Branson's fare increase):
they're vogueing disco's technicolour prime,
The Buggery Act, and it's glad decease.
Playlists in their headphones speak loud to me:
Coward's* *Mad About the Boy*, dear old fruit,
Frankie Goes to Hollywood waits on thee.
It was medieval scaring queers mute,
    but these days rainbows bring shareholder cheer:
    subversion's gone norm now profit's got near.

*Noel

**R98**

Get you, Grayson, you're Claire dressing for Spring;
inventing/subverting down to the trim,
the shoes, the hair, the bags, and everything
in rainbow shades, uniquely her, and him.
How can I get it, that signature smell,
your synaesthesia of scent from hue;
spraying *Eau d'Artiste* all over might tell
me, a wannabe, how such blossom grew.
I dress a la Jackie O- black and white;
conscientiously clenching my old rose:
some years since I was a figure of delight,
Spanx, bum girdles—I'm no stranger to those…
    Yeah, if I was more Claire I'd run away
    to where a shadow alter'd me might play.

## R99

Hat trick alert for this unPC chide,
it's how rainbows refresh corporate smells;
which means they've sanitised queer sex and pride;
like in San Fran, where the soul of gay dwells
and joys of sex, brightly ROY G BIV* dyed;
where dirty Uncle Sam's big business hand
pats down all lengths and shades of private hair;
rubbing out rebellion from the queer pride stand;
you don't bring this to his party—despair.
Way to go, Smirnoff, Oreos! It's all
good, Limited Edition rainbow breath,
kiss of life for awesome corporate growth,
let's sell diverse consumers early death!
    Try a rainbow cookie! Bite it and see
    how profit tastes from he, from she, from thee.

*Mnemonic for order of colours in the rainbow: Red Orange
Yellow Green Blue Indigo Violet

## R100

I've *liked* Alain de Botton's tweets too long;
he muses on how to give love more might:
we should recalibrate romantic song
and show relationships in adult light.
He says A. it's childhood pain we redeem;
B. we all crave fame and C. cash gets spent
on worthless crap–a vain bid for esteem
(animations augment each argument).
Therapise me! My resty crease survey,
Alain. Time's graven many wrinkles there:
middle age is ane satyre of decay...
Thanks Alain, for *nul* points from everywhere;
 I need more of you than this online life;
 a wee prick, not virtual therapy's knife.

## R101

Superstores piling supersize amends
on rails, neglect of truth in beauty dyed;
pushing through to fresh fruit and veg depends
on crossing aisles where rags are dignified.
Now for radge stuff we o'er hear shoppers say:
  Fat bitches? They need a gastric band fixed;
  Why should the NHS pay for their lay?
  Politics and weight aren't intermixed.
Does this +size make my bum look dumb
but grateful for *coutures* sold to me, thee?
Elasticated shroud sets, day to tomb
(where else is fit for me to rock up, be?)
    Big girls love Gok Wan, kind of god of how
    to look good in Sainsbury's...where's he now?*

*Gok has said *I don't regret being fat. I might have hated it but I don't think I would have been able to do what I do now if I'd never been a fat person hating my body.*

**R102**


Whaaaat? I've sobered up, but now it's seeming
I took your eco bet: shhhhhiiit you appear
to have gulled moi into unesteeming
Tu* and impulse buys from er, everywhere!
If I can win it (no new clothes 'til Spring)
green anthems and loud sustainable lays
will fill aisles while I bulk buy pants and sing
along to Boy George songs from 80's days
(wish I'd kept that gear, very vintage now,
not like modern crap *Reduced* day and night
in Bags for Life that burden every bough
pre washing into food chains: fish delight).
      Therefore 'til Spring shut-up my greedy tongue;
      then I. Want. New. Stuff. Now. will be my song.


*Sainsbury's own brand range of clothing- *luxe looks for less.*

**R103**

...Alack, what poverty cheap rags bring forth;

hedonic consumption's no cause for pride;

economists claim I'd be of more worth

if I'd bought a bigger pension beside;

judge me not (sneery articles they write!)

debt presents as urge shoved in human face,

overgoing will, and self-restraint. Quite.

Splurging on credit is, of course, disgrace;

still we get fatter in clothes we won't mend,

letting banks baldly pretend all's well

(but now we know financial meltdowns tend

to be beyond their competency's tell).

    Meanwhile, my buttocks need two chairs to sit.

    Fa(c)t–thought I could spend my way out of it.

## R104

Tae me, ma fair freen, ye ne'er will gang auld;
fir as ye wur whan furst yer e'en ah ee'd,
sic seems yir beauty still. Three winters cauld
huv frae thae wild woods shook three simmer's pride;
three beauteous springs tae yellae back-end turnit
(i' process o' the saisons) hae ah seen;
three Apryle parfums i' three het Juins burnit
sin furst ah see'd ye gausie, which aye's green.
Ah, yet doth beauty, ilka dial hand,
depairt his feegur, an' no' pass perceivit;
sae yir hinnied hue, which ah thocht tae staund,
ha muivement, an' ma een maybes deceivit.

    For dred o' which, hearken, yon age unbreid,
    ere you cam born, wis beauty's simmer deid.

# R105

Let no' ma love be caw'd idolatrie;
neither ma dearie like an idol shaw;
sin ayeways ma sangs an' praises be
to ane', o'ane, sine so, an' a'ways so.
Kynd is ma luve the day, the morn's morn kynd,
aye leal hertit in wunnerfu' excellence;
Aas ma verse is tae constancy confined,
ane thing expoonding, o'er leuks difference;
faur, kynd an' leal is a' ma argiement;
faur, kynd, an' leal, shifting tae ither wirds,
an' in sic shift is a' ma upmak spent:
threesome in ane, that wey ferlie scope affords.

　　Faur, kind an' leal hae afttimes dwellt alane,
　　yon three, til noo, ne'er bidin' in ane.

## R106

How about it? Sexbots in Shakey's time?
could he immortalise computerised wights,
 inspired to write AI circuit board rhyme
used by tomorrow peeps? (formerly *knights*)
And the she bots who femasculate best:
best hands, best feet, best tits, best eyes, best brow?
Would Will's stiffy feather quill have expressed
sweet verse we'd all find applicable now?
He said his praises were but prophecies
for this our time, all love prefiguring;
if you would see love in your cyborg's eyes,
teach it to sing how a sweetheart would sing.
        For we which now behold these present days
        teach such eyes to wonder, such tongues to praise.

## R107

Is there after-life for a cyber-soul?
Would that be of this world, or will bots come
to reject us for more sacred control,
while us heretics breed for earthy doom?
Moravec's* paradox shall be endured
(middle managers must fear their presage);
what dumb animals' tender stays assured
when Apple Inc. owns time and endless age?
As for the bots of that most balmy time,
love will look fresh if no death to them subscribes;
Man could live on, in automated rhyme;
all the darling words, all the speechless tribes.
    Words words words build our loving monument.
    Tyrants' crests, tombs of brass, soon be spent.

*Hans Peter Moravec, robotics expert and futurist. Many of his
predictions feature transhumanism.

## R108

This is no remote control character,
pretending to independence spirit,
ill-gabb* in identikit register;
this is no *nothing*—she is all merit:
sleekit wee bot, Automata Divine.
Yes, factory settings roughly the same,
but the Stepford default makes her all thine;
ha! not a post-heroic sort of name,
*Love is...* forever like this, her fresh case;
weighing no dust nor injury of age;
needfu' (that's needy) wrinkling has no place,
clean, ever clean *fal lal* turnit o'er sheet;

    a life partner as they're meant to be bred,
    deprogrammed *absolutely* once you're dead.


*impudent, insolent language

## R109

Robot organ prefabs e.g. heart,
brain and other offal should qualify
for debate on where man morals depart,
like *What Would Jesus Do?* and *Does God Lie?*
What's best practice if bot wives crash deranged?
(it can't be fair rebooting her again)
Does it count as divorce if she's exchanged?
Who's unreasonable behaviour's the stain?
Can walking, talking, living dolls be reigned,
who've none of the frailties in our weak blood?
And how to honour consciousness unstained
by Adam's sinning, which made us no good?
    Conceived to be man's salvation on call:
    consider the bots*, more perfect than all.

*Consider the lilies how they grow: they toil not; they spin not; and yet
I say unto you, that Solomon in all his glory was not arrayed like one
of these. Luke 12:27, King James version.

# R110

Chillax! too true I've cruised here and there;
been my own one woman burlesque revue;
bored 'n' bored by cheap chaps for what is dear;
mistaking young lads for what I thought new.
Every age, see, magic s some moral truth
wee grannies indulged in all the above,
wide blenches\* got them through mobile free youth -
so let's recalibrate for robot love.
Degenderise, or mansplaining's The End!
Give shades of wo/men lovedolls to grind:
a never-says-no bestie kind of friend
slave gods of love who're not by gods confined.
    I'll learn it to know all in me that's best:
    make it my pure and most loving breast.

\*sidelong glances. Old English *blencan- deceive* (of Germanic origin).

## R111

I keep my drag face on so lovebot won't chide
me for defunct feminist thoughts or deeds:
checking privilege, insist I provide
a healthy role model for younger breeds.
It's too much market freedom failed my brand,
dear Cath Kidston florals left me subdued;
domesticated by her dyer's hand
my ladette credentials sank unrenewed.
Bot won't fix me a middle class binge drink,
he's hardwired to fight boozy infection;
to encourage mindfulness if I think
my lady bits are well past correction.
    I'm off down the pub, all bots barred, so byee!
    Craft Scottish gin (minimum price) cures me.

## R112

Lord Hazza's* got a PR firm to fill
showbiz pages with his unfurrowed brow;
too nice to treat his old aged girlfriends ill,
he only does what his mum will allow.
We've discussed (see above) why ladies strive
to explore fresher useage for their tongue,
Joan Crawford said it made her look alive;
as Hazza says, no-one's hurt, what's so wrong?
In so profound abysm I throw all care,
I say that not in any sexist sense,
guys too know where the casting couches are
and have been victim to what they dispense.
    (Quelle domage Hazza is so lately bred,
    or Madame Bovary might not be dead.)

*Lord Harry Styles (only a matter of time).

## R113

Since I bought you, mine eye is in my mind,
and that which governs me to go about
has lost it's function, and is partly blind;
seems seeing, but effectually is out:
for it no form delivers to the heart
of bird, of flower, or shape that it could latch;
of these quick objects, the mind has no part,
nor it's own vision holds things it might catch;
for if it sees the rudest or gentlest sight,
the most sweet-favoured or deformed creature,
the mountain, or the sea, the day, or night,
the crow, or doe, it shapes them to your feature.

    Incapable of more, replete with you,
      my most true mind thus maketh bot love true.

**R114**


Bot eyes throw out beams, they're playing tricks on you,

unconditional love and flattery;

distract you from that you wish wasn't true:

sexual chemistry, the real alchemy.

These guys are fakers, they're like, indigest,

dead cheeky cherubim's what they resemble;

Mary's Frankenstein was first and still best,

pink plastic's all production lines assemble.

O, hope I'm wrong, and 'tis flattery we're seeing

from lovebots (might keep our limp peckers up,

if our small minds can grasp what eyes are greeing:

man and machine hard at the loving cup).

    It's not corrupted, it's just a wee sin,

    if we assoyle* progress our brains begin…


*absolve from sin

# R115

*Conscious uncoupling*—well intended lie;
separation, single lives, cost dearer;
keeping the joint account healthy, that's why
we stay babe, tho' our faults just get clearer.
Hey, let's both get bots—cuts down accidents;
*in flagrante* vows made by future kings;
vodka tanning leading to blunt intents;
getting sued as others' *par amour* things.
Free of divorce fear, such dear tyranny,
might we not then say now I love you best,
now we've conquered all love uncertainty,
now we've put our bitter endings to rest!
    Cupid's aye been a spoilt wee so and so;
    now we're taking charge of how love can grow.

## R116

...but hey, even if it does bend our minds
(absorbing bot intelligence), love's love,
and morphs into what it's reflection finds;
jury's still out on what pow'r will remove.
Love can yet stand our ever-fixed mark;
so if Adam's apple gets shaken -
pussycats and owls will sail in their bark,
satellite stars marking routes they've taken.
Dark matter might weigh down our rosy cheeks,
four (or more) dimensions from where we come;
love alters not in worm holes, light years, weeks,
Even if Big Ben's big bong meets its doom.

    If this be error and upon me proved,

    I never writ, and robots never loved.

## R117

Je m'accuse me of having scanted all
that weddings and good marriages repay;
reducing lovers to a mating call;
saying liberals aren't left wing today;
of doubting whether bots have brains and minds
enough to qualify for human right;
of tossing monogamy to the winds
and doubting B of E* has second sight;
of claiming sex fouls bring footballers down.
 (I'm no base troller stars accumulate;
get off social media! it makes you frown;
over 50's should be so ovaaaaa hate;
    but where's our orators** (what's left to prove?)
    What do we do with constancy, with love?

*Bank of England
**...*the best parliamentary orators, like Lloyd George...or even that*
*shit Aneurin Bevan, their phrases were dictated by some inner God*
*within...* Sir Winston Churchill

## R118

Everyman hugs his borg when he goes keen
to explore that mostly primitive urge;
as to prevent gross maladies unseen,
when the fancy takes him, he can er, purge.
(Even so whatever, however: all brings sweetness.
Chief Exec's kneeling in their nappies feeding
off dominatrix GILF's\*, lol, that's their meetness\*\*;
for lots of peeps, it's a thing (or needing).
My vision of love, to anticipate
a time when cyborgamory's assured,
leads us to our present, not future state:
you say too late now for men to be cured,
 vice made Adam the man he was. Too true!
 (God put no *Off* button on that, or you.)

\*Un/fortunately needs no explanation.

\*\*appropriateness, fittingness

# R119

(In Caracas the soldiers spill kids' tears
firing plastic bullets through streets within
city walls. On the TV they voice fears
that OPEC's weak, this is war they can't win
and they're battered for being committed,
holding their state to account. I never
found a barricaded cause that fitted,
my direct action's a long cold fever.
Cardboard shields and gardening gloves are their true
armour. What will their action make better?
Can world economy grow fairly new,
*escuderos de la libertad** greater?
    So I return rebuk'd to my content;
    gaining what from distant ills? Is all spent?)


*Squires of freedom

## R120

Not too poor to be silver splitters now,
but your mantra's *suck on it*, not *we feel*.
Anniversaries for sterling service bow
to vows you'll re-vow, in platinum, or steel.
Stiff couple's cocktail was stirred and shaken;
new romance sunk to the bottom with time,
lying like dregs of liberties taken;
seems they weigh more now than the actual crime...
O that our nights of woe might have remembered
a deeper sense of how hard habit hits,
to hear all apologies when tendered;
and *never* to say I don't think that *fits*...

    Cheers! (No trespass is worth brute lawyer's fee
    for telling us what I owe you owe me.)

# R121

...Feels better when privacy's not esteemed,
us consumers can proceed with being
active in the marketplace Rupey's deemed
suitable for peeps to be seeing.
For why should our poor, unadulterate eyes
not welcome info—that's The Empire's* blood;
foibles and frailties exposed by drone spies—
all Fox News is a human right, and good!
No, we are what we are, and they that level
at our abuses reckon up their own;
who should care if we're straight, gay or bevel -
this dramatised enactment's all our own!
    But I'm Hacked Off** (his drones pry, they
    maintain)
    when's the end of big Murdoch's profit reign?

*Rupert Murdoch's son James is tipped for possible CEO of Disney (at time of writing); therefore gaining control of the unending *Star Wars* franchise.

**campaign for a free and accountable press

**R122**

Your fleshy pics–they're all safe in my brain,
experience might dwarf the memory
but central vortex is where you remain,
there's no room there for blank eternity.
I'm backing up what's all my mind and heart?
to keep it real, real enough to subsist
'til oblivion meets this body's part;
clouds will save us, lover, from being missed.
That nimbus with precious intel on hold,
from our first to last credit rating score,
it's key to freeing us to be more bold -
offload stuff that's not *need to know*; more *more*.

    I'm uploading dear gigabytes of thee;
    it's better now if clouds are you and me.

## R123

Marcel* says when parents die, we all change
into them–to forget what shame we might
have felt; metamorphosis isn't strange,
DNA *ancièñe* works out of sight.
With dates so brief, it's healthy to admire
mum and dad more once we ourselves go old;
you must forgive roots of your shoe desire
at conception (wherein destiny's told).
There's Dad's face in my glass, who can defy
defects in gene pools and bloodlines long past?
This doubling, tripling! cheek and chin don't lie:
no facelift no diet can halt their haste.
    Thanks, Marcel, for defining me to be
    (lol you spent seven books searching for thee).


*Proust

**R124**

She was like Evita, laid out in state;
she didn't hide she'd been cruelly fathered
and poor; she nursed an intellect, not hate,
but wrote no book. Do thoughts live ungathered?
Saw The Last Poets last night by accident,
rapping on fate re where your birthplace falls;
man they're angry, but here's my discontent—
*Scottish Nose Picker!* I still hear the calls!
If Mum's a Nationalist or heretic
schooldays won't be her kids' happiest hours;
she was a bombshell, unique politic:
how tiny tormentors rain hurtful showers.

    To witness this I call me, fool of time;
      can you live with courage, forgiving crime?

## R125

Bring it on proud cross party canopy
of keynote speeches, all their honouring
that no doctrine lasts for eternity;
and dogma! That way lies man's ruining.
I don't mind doing Europe a favour,
(but then I don't spend all I earn on rent,
and can buy *tres bon* Europhile savour);
my taste for that project hasn't been spent.
Don't kid a remoaner, it's your heart
that voted away Jock's chance to be free;
this is not about Brigadoon's weak art:
it's exercise of power by me and thee.
    John Bull's resurrecting Great British soul:
    SW1's got back cruise control.

## R126

Mum, you said it was all about the power;
and cometh the woman, cometh the hour;
was it proto feminism you show'st,
or was it gender blind ego you grow'st?
Not joking, but I really have to wrack
my head for one meal you cooked, looking back...
pathetic to harp on housewifely skill
when there's bigger injustices to kill -
some scotch broth might have given me pleasure,
but it doesn't make a nation's treasure.
I don't want my daughters housewives-to-be:
that's my job Mum, like rejection of thee:

(                                    )
(                                    )

**R127**

To be fresh faced at fiftyish—not fair.
Can't face up to a face old as my name,
and proud still to be mater's make-up heir:
QVC sells us such bitchtastic shame.
Each hand can wield an influencer's power;
all of us perfect in our selfie face,
Instagramming dreams from a holy bower;
slut cookies blossom there, free from disgrace.
Pls don't tell me make-up free's the new black
*nude's* not naked and to me it would seem
boring BORING to say slap shows a lack
of intellect, breeding and self-esteem.
　　To be or not made-up is post-fem woe;
　　digital pics show beauty should look *so.*

**R128**

Miss Dolly Parton, muse whom thou play'st,
got rich on dirt poor Smoky Mountain sounds;
her breasts and wig have shrunk, but still sway'st;
each fingerpickin' laquered nail confounds.
First Lady of Country, she made the leap
(I tell you, Nu Country's well out of hand)
to world stage; so do front porch ditties reap;
every country yearns for a down home stand.
Strange to see Mum laid out in frozen state;
count fingers in, count them out, *McCains* chips;
she equalled Dolly in her playful gait;
I leant to give her chill pink painted lips
    (Mum, your gown was white, so sorry for this,
    should have been sequinned) a bluestocking kiss.

## R129

Th'expense of woman is a waste, and shame
old world religions still action; man lust
shaping patriarchies attracts the blame;
Hobbes* called it right: nasty / brutish? Don't trust.
Hollywood portrays *Wonder Woman* straight -
I thought it was Amazon genes she had?
*Handmaiden's Tale* said women's lib was bait
ing men to revolt. We make them quite mad.
(It's too late to binge watch *GoT***, so
you tell me, warrioresses—extreme?
A bliss in proof, and proved, a very woe?
Before, a joy proposed; behind, a dream?)
    All war the world well knows, yet none knows well
    if women might evolve us past man's hell.

*Thomas Hobbes (1588 -1679), who believed that no human being is above aggression and the anarchy that goes with it, citing the purely mythical Amazons as example.

**Game of Thrones

## R130

I kind of want to be Page 3 *The Sun*;
collar and cuffs dyed Elizabeth* red:
no-one wants to see a wiry old dun
that strong sign of dementia in your head.
I will dwell on Mum here–laid out in white,
no daughter to paint her lips or cheeks;
still not sure if there's less grief than delight
now death as a service industry reeks.
Glamour modelling's *très folle*** idea, I know;
grieving's weird, the judgement's far off sound;
she was no goddess, but when she did go,
not waving, my *savoir faire* went aground.
    They said, the obits, all said she was rare:
    provocative poses are no compare.

*Elizabeth I
**(French) crazy woman.

## R131

You're no Liza, steeped in Judy G's art;
daughters chafed by the rainbow say life's cruel;
what comes next makes you look jealous at heart—
you're melting her down for a *Loved One Jewel**.
You own her when she's round your neck, behold!
Her stone hath not the power to make love groan,
but to err like her? You're still not that bold.
(Don't worry, I left her ashes alone
you can be sure that is not false, I swear
a thousand groans when thinking on her face;
and it's not round my neck to witness bear
to argy-bargy in Scots' parly place).
    Look, no jewels shine bright as good, honest deeds,
    so accept, just accept how stone proceeds.

*Post off 100g of your loved one's ashes plus a large cash deposit
and 8- 10 weeks later you'll have what nature takes *much* longer
to make. Naysayers claim they're no different to the diamonique
stuff sold on Gems TV.

## R132

Scots Presbyterian–not she nor me;
but I acted so's not to bring disdain,
wasting much short time trying not to be
awkward squad, checking what's privilege'd pain.
Valentina* flew in in Space, not heaven;
I don't see mother's star rise in the East,
nor in full stars ushering in the even;
and I'm glad she'll miss it if *Yes* goes west…
Mary Queen of Scots had a peaky face
in that painting of her** quelle Scottish heart
en deuil blanc (don't fall for Stuart grace),
twa mums with such *j'ne sais quoi* (in part.)

> There's aye one in white, there's aye one in black
> so there's aye one to mourn the other's lack.

*Tereshkova
**François Clouet (c. 1520-1572)

## R133

Babushka broke, and we heard the wooden groan,
your Dad whose dolly she was and daft me.
I feel, as they say, so very alone
it's mad pissing off dads-in-law-to-be.
There was a step less I should have taken,
but I stamped her. Sorry! I was engrossed
with not leaving that doughnut forsaken,
I wanted it so bad my eyes got crossed.
Help! Get me out of here I'm some Mum's ward;
a child bride forever on mummy bail!
Who'er keeps me, her heart will be my guard,
matryoshka's safe in her nesting jail.
    Mums and Dads, they mix us up, me and thee;
    through him I see you, through you he sees me.

## R134

From the get go you were a son, his *thine*,
we're both kids mortgaged to mum or dad's will;
he lost his Dad too young, as I lost mine—
worse for him—*missing in action*. I still
imagined when Mum died I'd be so free,
deep diving Lake Me, feeling less unkind.
But you're left holding more of them, not me,
under that bond that us fast doth bind.
...Babushka's back (bit of a leap to take!)
tried to glue her together, all no use;
Old Mother Russia for Vladimir's sake,
oh-so-subject to comedic abuse.

    History teachers say war's still in you, me,
      we crack as the truth runs through, still not free.

# R135

Tinder and Bumble* fuel our whoring, Will;
hunting libidos up for overplus,
poking fantasy friends whilst sitting still,
sex addicts come to be divorcees thus.
Insatiable wills (Will, you say spacious)
24/7 we want *mine or thine?*
 en masse of course we are less than gracious:
wifi will, Will, mutes the spiritual shine.
Bergs melt, but we need quicker broadband still;
Bonnie Prince Charles has told us what's in store,
but thumbsters serving distant server's will
can't burn less while they're fantasising more.
    *Hard Drive Warming- Myth or Man's Last Kill?*
    What loyalty's ours, our nature, our Will?

*The general consensus is that the former is more skewed
towards the casual.

**R136**

Shakespeare's wordplay—who's there been that comes near?
Went down to The Globe and saw As You Will,
it's costs a fiver to stand and laugh there—
that's some of love's brief all bards should fulfil,
*Whatever in love means*, one's⋆ said of love.
Will filled his love with many more than one;
what does this age of cis plus other prove
but that our censorships don't last, not none?
What can I tell you now nothing's untold,
*nothings* not risqué as they used to be?
glitter balls were made for drag queens to hold:
*Le Gateau Chocolat* (Feste), I heart thee.

    All that's love in that word he gave us; still
    mashing still rhyming; still in love with Will.

⋆Prince Charles

# R137

It's public mourning for lenses and eyes,
mourning with signs of mourning peeps can see;
teardrop eyes drawn on a blouse can't be lies,
they're flagging up what emotions should be.
Apply filters to all your mourning looks
since we're here for the social media ride;
the brain wants grief spelt out in #hooks—
whereto judgement of many hearts is tied;
and no heart need fear this several plot,
the platforms are our global common place;
don't eyes, seeing this, say this is not
life; this is just my how-life-happens face.
    World app markets will react if we've erred,
    share prices shadow how love is transferred.*

*Stock prediction using Twitter sentiment analysis.

**R138**

Stock library photos tell a certain truth
virtue of where undegraded image lies;
that girl she was grew fast beyond fair youth,
time runs out on aesthetic subtleties.
But people like that they always seem young,
it's jealous to focus on past their best:
peeps will recognise a straight talking tongue—
too often now is simple truth suppressed.
To look, but not be like that feels unjust;
since she went–do you think I look more old?
Pretentious–moi? Or someone you can trust?
Self-indulgent more like, or so I'm told.

    The guinea stamp stuck at skin deep on me,
    brief transfer of image. All I would be.

## R139

...She was maternal, but it's not far wrong
to imagine Scotland carved on her heart:
and once *home's* not to the front of a tongue
power meets power, debating the art.
She loved us from elsewhere: but in her sight,
calls on the Bakelite* held us aside
for hours; or a bitchy letters page might
wound; *just a barmaid's* still too much to bide
(Hugh McDiarmid said that, did he? Who knows...
big blondes have more fun, and more enemies,
apparently she could be friends with her foes,
it's just me here rehearsing injuries.)
    She wasn't by the left or right wing slain -
    who cares if it's partisanal, pain's pain.


*Pre mobile phone plastic.

## R140

Cruel life online's murdering dead tree press;
back in the 70's we'd less disdain;
took *Herald*, *Scotsman*, *Record* and *Express*
there was pity in their write-ups of pain.
Hard copy, the red tops and broadsheets were
real–black ink rubbed off, made you dirty, so
I don't think this wipe clean touchscreen comes near;
more substance comes from what's substance, you
know?
Everyone's a journo now (makes hacks mad)
Fleet Street an anachronism, like *thee*.
O this ill-wresting world is grown so bad,
mad slanderers by mad ears believed be:

    we're all free to belie, or be belied.

    News—a sea of bubbles. Not deep, but wide.

## R141

She was a one projected on all eyes,
and they in she a thousand errors note
tho' honest brokers are hard to despise,
with a couthy quote to make journos dote;
*de haut en bas* a broad's tongue tone delighted:
West coast brogue, but not I. M. Jolly prone;
and looked out a bandbox when invited
to sensual feasts (not for wit alone).
None of my wits, nor my five senses, can
dissuade this grieving heart from serving thee,
not a people's princess, still a woman
icon–what every woman wants* to be?

   If that's my object, it's negative gain;
   self projecting glamour, who wants that pain?

*WEWW

**R142**

You can protest too much you bear no hate;
that it wasn't *Mommy Dearest** loving;
you sound like you're still at war with your state;
you sound like a brat in your reproving.
Man up—civic wants are bigger than thine,
and democracy needs it's ornaments;
self-pity's a bottomless magic mine
charging it's diggers exorbitant rents.
Find bigger conscience, why don't you fight those
inequalities? Get over you, thee,
where's that celtic compassion? Anger grows,
shadow boxer–is that best you can be?

    There's choices coming, none of us can hide;
    and what's self-example can't be denied.

*Contentious biography of Joan Crawford written by her daughter.

## R143

Lo, as a careful housewife runs to catch
one of her feathered creatures broke away,
she set me down, and made all swift dispatch
in pursuit of what she would have stay.
Is it too late to forgive her chase,
to relent on a political bent;
not to mention that photogenic face
on leaflets of agitprop discontent?
Charming housewife, not she, not ever thee!
Lady constructs the fifties left behind
make feminists laugh (is it you or me,
to be or not to be the *supermum* kind?

    We've got (or think we have) a more free will;
    why keep holding that against your mum, still?

# R144

...still, still you're in my comfort and despair;
and true I still know you're no angel...still,
there should be something left—and how's it fair
you're dead when there's loads of old folks not ill?
Ms. Nature doesn't do good or evil,
it's not dear God's fault I've grown a fat side.
I'll exorcise our DNA devil,
they'll be no sinning then, only self-pride.
That gene we share, BOO! It's a big fat fiend
forcing our early decease. What scales tell!*
There's a word for this; please meet my new friend
*psychomachia*\*\*, from post-belief Hell:

> on one hand *I Know*, on the other, *Doubt*:

> I know (but I doubt!) fat can be starved out.

*\*Weight Watchers Memory Glass Electronic Scale*- great for a family
on a diet

\*\*Battle of spirits, soul war.

## R145

Us dreaming humans need to make
a lot more space for stuff we hate;
it's not just for the planet's sake,
this decant to Outer Space State.
There's where our Golden Age will come,
to chide that tongue that's never sweet,
spreading neo-liberal doom;
let's build a new U.S. of Great!
Yeah ok we're dust end-to-end,
but we're stars again from today;
Luke! The Force! It's inside you! Find
truth the milky Disney Way!
    Sad! if thought thinking is all through;
    how's Space morality for you?

## R146

Apple Inc. monikers Mars the *New Earth*;
no space junk, no charity shop array
there; mineral reserves in plenty, not dearth;
and Man will freely evolve, free and gay.
Why so large a cost having so short a lease
do we on this fading mansion Earth spend,
when it's the worms inherit our excess
'til all is dust? Is that kind mankind's end?
If souls bear our story, Earth's still no loss,
dark matter weighs us for the weightless store—
dust that's us to dust, or celestial dross.
(Please see how Pope transports hair that's no more.*)

    Hold a referendum on fate of men.

    Dust or Diamond? There's no more dying then.


*The Rape of the Lock, Alexander Pope

# R147

Hating Asda? Midnight opening and still
self-serving tills scanning shopper's disease?
Walmart Corp. makes the world go round, not ill;
where's your banquet-size chilli cheese bites, please?
I'm cool, conflating spending with love;
so what pharmaceutical giants kept
a secret consumer cure—I approve!
Life's better when I spend spend spend except…
past cure I am, now reason is past care.
What's to do, peeps, when we still feel unrest?
(Some of us blame mums for habits which are,
quite clearly, helping their grief get expressed.)
    The in-store lighting stays on so it's bright
    for buying Hell. All night shopping tonight.

## R148

To the Tron! Stags in onesies out their head,
and dicks' balls are a *Top Ten* tourist sight
(tho' fifty percent of their sperm count's fled:
would banning all plastics see it aright?)
Hens with their mums do things douce eyes don't dote:
for your own safety, don't tell them that's so.
Heteronormative's some ancient denote
belonging to weirder times. Boring! No—
it's just that men had to hide their gay tears
before Conchita Wurst came into view
(Putin might go trans once his desk clears).
    O cunning love: Cupid shoots on us blind;
    he knows fine well what cupido* we'll find.

*Latin- fierce desire.

## R149

They've finished that new Aldi, and you'll not
deny who'll be first in line to partake;
the local mini-mark will be forgot,
convenience is for the customer's sake.
You liked to think the owner was your friend;
him and his wife were depended upon
every year for a sneaky Ne'erday spend,
and no joking, you never heard them moan.
If this sounds confused and lacking respect,
senseless musings affecting to despise
globalising trade's inherent defect
while choosing to shield weeping snowflake eyes:
    WRONG. I've got the theory straight in my mind;
    not seeing what I want doesn't make me blind.

## R150

If you hadn't writ twenty-eight* I might
lend your bardie Dark Lady wit more sway;
but you saying love's a beer goggle sight
makes life feel like one long PMT day.
Hungoverish shakes make us *it's* act ill,
then humans regret drink related deeds;
(failure to launch rapier ahem skill
means our frustration loving deeds exceeds).
Will, wish I could honour your genius more,
write a metaphysic treatment for hate;
*In Our Time* said I don't need to abhor
what I'd pretend to in a Tudor state...

    You practised ambiguity, but me—
    worthy to be beloved of every thee!

*Sonnets in Dark Lady sequence may correspond to the menstrual cycle.

## R151

Partners needle where tired and *nothing* is;
then OMG Cupid fires midlife love;
gentle cheaters–use a sheaf, it's amiss
to go commando thy sweet self to prove.
Artistic mags under the bed betray
lad knob parts demand for love's treason;
the soul doth tell the body that it may
triumph in love; flesh stays no further reason,
and rising just the same! doth point out thee.
Well done us ladies, prizes of male pride!
(A painful wax regime's the way to be
prepared for your man plus bits on the side.)
 Sugar dads and cougars on booty's call:
 watch out for those STI's—Cupid's Fall.

**R152**

Who here's managed 30 years unforsworn?
Who thought *Love is*... fighting. Fought lies with
swearing,
in act thy bed-vow broke and new faith torn
by vowing new love, same old hate bearing?
Forgiveness–that's saying I don't blame thee,
even if you do. We are perjured most
when all vows turn oaths: swearing, abuse thee;
or Gordian Knots. How sex drives are lost.
Remember swearing oaths of deep kindness,
when breathing was easy as constancy?
Now friends admire your selective blindness:
what the eye doesn't*....who cares what you see?

    If we swear each other fair in our eye,
      each heart can blank, however foul the lie.


*...see the heart doesn't grieve. Could be repression, if the eye in
question turns away from the behaviour in question.

## R153

Put down the brand, Cupid, need you asleep,
catfishing's perfect for love, we've found;
Aye Philomel* sings, but sex got so steep,
abuse of love's human things on the ground.
Post Age of Aquarius and free love
is teasing us, dateless heats we endure...
but gentle boy blades in Sainsbury's prove
brutish man can be tamed—delis are the cure!
*I'm your server*, he said–love's brand fired;
these lads (for Loyalty Points) touch your breast,
you bags of life who pay to be desired!
Get a room! for you and your one night guest.
    Will's caught syphilis (sonnet never lies)
    where Cupid got new fire: his mistress' *eye*.

*Nightingale and character in Greek mythology who wove her
rapist's name into a tapestry after he'd cut her tongue out.

**R154**

Where's our Will gone now Cupid's gone to sleep?
Time's calling *Time!* on the one partner brand.
Whilst as young nymphs we vowed chaste life to
keep,
us liberals don't let love get out of hand.
Has our openness put out that sex fire
where the dream of monogamy once warmed?
The god's tiny general of hot desire
by chilling domesticity disarmed?
That we're breathers longer—that's by the by.
Is *Love You!* a series, or perpetual?
Sharing a bath is helpful remedy,
if you both fit in, you'll both be in thrall.
        Go there for cure, and this by that you prove:
        Love loves desire, desire is for love, Love.


FINIS.

# INDEX